SHEENA SWEET

The Power to Transform

Breaking free by stepping into the new with God establishing your identity in Christ

Copyright © 2024 by Sheena Sweet

All rights reserved. No part of this publication may be reproduced, stored or transmitted in any form or by any means, electronic, mechanical, photocopying, recording, scanning, or otherwise without written permission from the publisher. It is illegal to copy this book, post it to a website, or distribute it by any other means without permission.

First edition

ISBN: 979-8-218-53879-8

This book was professionally typeset on Reedsy. Find out more at reedsy.com

Contents

1 Introduction 1
2 Acceptance 3
3 Repentance 7
4 Surrender 12
5 Foundation 15
6 Restructured 18
7 Faith 23
8 Dedication 28

1

Introduction

Romans 12:2

"Don't copy the behavior and customs of this world, but let God transform you into a new person by changing the way you think. Then you will learn to know God's will for you, which is good and pleasing and perfect."

The Power to transform takes place when men embrace the will of God. Establishing Christ as their foundation. They embrace the guidance of the Holy Spirit in every aspect of their lives. Realizing that real transformation is the result of God taking away the old man for the new man to take center stage; things that were out of alignment with God had to be eliminated such as control, rebellion, unforgiveness, anger and other traits. Becoming closer to God by following his decrees and regulations, having faith, and trusting in God's process. This transformation leads to experiencing God's glory and wisdom, witnessing His work in one's life. Resulting in remarkable changes that inspire others.

Father, in the name of Jesus, I pray that each reader of this book is enlightened with a deeper understanding of who You are. El Elohim, the one and only true living God, who has the power to transform and guide Your children back to Your original plan; if they are willing to surrender and let

THE POWER TO TRANSFORM

You in. Father, let their eyes be opened to all truth and not be deceived by false doctrine. Show them how You have transformed my life for the better, and that such transformation is possible for them as well. Lastly, Father, I pray they will know and experience Your unfailing love
Amen!

2

Acceptance

John 3:16

"For God so loved the world that he gave his one and only Son, that whoever believes in him shall not perish but have eternal life."

Growing up as a young girl, I knew of God. But I didn't know Him or fully understand His laws and regulations. Like most people, I went to church, praised God, and heard the word without any intentions of reading or understanding the Bible for myself. My excuse was that the Bible is "too thick" or it has "too many pages." Yeah, I know, pure laziness, right? It's like I had time for everything else but God. Because I knew I had a praying grandmother and aunt who would intercede and cover me in their prayers. Let's be honest; all of us have experienced times when we depended on the divine relationship of our parents, grandparents, relatives, or friends to justify our sinful nature. This reliance prevents us from experiencing a true partnership, relationship, and understanding with God for ourselves. We are meant to be fruitful and increase in number, fill the earth and subdue it, and rule over the fish in the sea, the birds in the sky, and every living creature that moves on the ground, as (Genesis 1:28) commands us. However, we often become stubborn and choose to do things our own way, being led by the flesh instead of the Holy Spirit that we have access to when we come into the acceptance of Jesus Christ as our Lord and Savior

You see, while living in sin ,I felt everything was okay until I crashed in life experiences with no hope or an expected future. This forced me to make a decision on whom I would serve. "For no one can serve two masters; for either he will hate the one and love the other, or he will stand by and be devoted to the one and despise and be against the other. You cannot serve God and mammon—deceitful riches, money, possessions, or whatever is trusted in" (Matthew 6:24). You may be wondering, "How would I know who I am serving?" Let me explain. God is for peace, giving, helping, and love, while we live a righteous life. On the other hand, Satan believes the complete opposite: hate, violence, confusion, and that it is better to receive than to give. The differences between these two spirits are very clear. Basically, we can serve God, who sets us free from sin, or Satan, who enslaves us to the worldly mindset—money, lust, pride, anger, fornication, etc. As you should know, God is a spirit, and we must worship Him in spirit and truth (John 4:24). We must also understand that everything we go through in life is spiritual. And yes, Satan is a spirit too. But we will "NOT" glorify him in any way.

I can definitely tell you that I was lost and didn't even know I was headed towards death and destruction. Without realizing that everything I experienced was spiritual, and I was contributing to my own troubles by staying in sin. How many of us are like that? Clueless! Moving through life on our own "will" without peace and constant confusion, wondering why or questioning God. We don't realize it was all a part of the enemy's plan to destroy us and cause us to place blame on God. All because our flesh was not under control, nor were our minds aligned with Christ. Let's be honest, the first thing we all scream out with frustration is, "Oh God! Why did you do this to me?" Well, sometimes it is not God; it is you and your natural desires that have consequences. We sometimes make it so easy for the devil because of our ignorance. That's the part I had to learn and recognize on whom I was serving, Satan (The World) or God.

ACCEPTANCE

It took me hitting rock bottom where I felt alone, hurt and disappointed in life. Yes, I had people to talk to. But, they could never provide the comfort I needed or peace to subdue all the pain and emptiness I was feeling inside. When I received advice from relatives and friends, it was from a worldly standpoint that would have left me crippled if I had listened. But there was one relative, my sister-in-law, who spearheaded me into this journey of living a righteous life fully surrendered to God. She would always say, "Go to God and open that Bible." So, I decided to give God a try. One evening, as I was crying out to God, ready to give up on life completely, He revealed Himself to me. He said, "Get up! You will not stay in this rut, and you were never alone". The only reason why I felt alone was because I never invited him into all areas of my life, marriage, finances, raising my daughter, family, career and relationships. This became the light switch moment for me; so I decided to turn my life over to Christ; choosing Life realizing that this is far greater than me. (Deuteronomy 30:19) reminds me that " He calls heaven and earth as witnesses today against us, *that* he has set before us life and death, blessing and cursing; therefore choose life, that both you and your descendants may live." This was the only way for me to receive peace and comfort through Jesus Christ as my Lord and Savior.

Where there is therefore now no condemnation for those who are in Christ Jesus as (Romans 8:1) reminds us. What is condemnation, you may ask? It is the expression or act of strong disapproval or criticism such as pride, worry, fear, doubt, discouragement, depression, hopelessness, and every sin that easily besets us from experiencing God's plan for our lives. But once we come into His truth and knowledge, He sets us free from all of it. I used to be very hard on myself because of the life choices I have made, and that is not what He expects for us to do.(Luke 15:7) confirms to us that "There will be more joy in heaven over one sinner who repents, than over ninety-nine righteous people who have no need of repentance" So, you see God and Heaven gets excited when we make the right step towards Him. With a promise that He will forgive our iniquities and will no longer remember our sins (Hebrews 8:12). Though your life may be completely upside down at the moment, you have the option to choose to accept Jesus Christ as your Lord and Savior, as I did today, in order to start over and become a new man.

Prayer To Accept Jesus Christ As Your Lord and Savior
"Dear Heavenly Father, I know that I am a sinner, and I ask for your forgiveness. I believe you died for my sins and rose from the dead. I turn from my sins and invite you to come into my heart and life. I want to trust and follow you as my Lord and Savior."
Amen!

3

Repentance

Galatians 5 19 - 21

"The acts of the sinful nature are obvious: sexual immorality, impurity and debauchery; idolatry and witchcraft; hatred, discord, jealousy, fits of rage, selfish ambition, dissensions, factions and envy; drunkenness, orgies, and the like. I warn you, as I did before, that those who live like this will not inherit the kingdom of God."

Can you imagine going through life thinking you're right about everything? Without realizing that God was trying to get your attention in so many ways; but, yet you failed to see it because of pride and temptation. Have you ever been in a situation where you were oblivious to the warnings or you chose to ignore them? Then later on say "OH" that was a red flag! That was me for a very long time. My pride and temptation drove me into ruins, and brought me to an abrupt end. I would say, like most, that God is tempting me. But, that was further from the truth. You see, God will never try to trip us up. He is impervious to evil, and puts evil in no one's way. The temptation to give in to evil comes from us and only us. We have no one to blame but the leering, seducing flare-up of our own lust. Lust gets pregnant, and has a baby: sin! Sin grows up to adulthood, and becomes a real killer. Through my ignorance and curiosity; I opened up so many doors to the enemy by living according to the world standards. I thought it was Ok to seek fortune tellers, worship ancestors, fornicate ,idolize, and the list goes on. Allow me to elaborate on why the wages of my sins meant death for me if I continued.

The moment I sought a fortune teller and worshiped false gods, my life became chaotic from that day forward. Where my home was under attack- to me facing separation and divorce to my daughter and I constantly arguing along with confusion on the job. To be honest, whenever I spoke to a fortune teller it never felt right all the way to the pit of my belly. But I dismissed that feeling because I just had to know. In the midst of this, I was even told that I should leave my husband by a fortune teller. But it was my husband who left instead. Talk about straight- up confusion and deception that fell upon me. I mean, the fact that I didn't know it was against God's laws and regulations was not an excuse. For it was my responsibility to read his word so that I would not be deceived or fall prey to the enemy devices. "For My people are destroyed for lack of knowledge. Because you have rejected knowledge, I also will reject you from being priest for me. Because you have forgotten the law of your God. I will also forget your children" (Hosea 4:6). This was the turning point in my life when I began to fade away and, regretfully, fall into despair, plunging more and further into the dark. It seemed as though God was showing me a candle in the middle of the road once lit, that had now been blown out.

So, when people tell you, "Try out the fortune tellers. Consult the spiritualists. Why not tap into the spirit-world and get in touch with the dead?"Tell them, "No, you are going to study Scriptures." People who try other ways get nowhere but a dead end! Frustrated and famished, they try one thing after another. When nothing works out for them, they get angry, cursing their king and their God. Looking this way and that, up, down, and sideways and see nothing. But a blank wall, an empty hole. They end up in the dark with nothing. Would you believe this is scripture? Absolutely, it is (Isaiah 8:19). Let me go on further to inform you that the dead have nothing to do with the living, they are consulting a familiar spirit, which is not of God to deceive you. (Leviticus 20: 6-7) warns us what will happen "The person who turns to mediums and familiar spirits, to prostitute himself with them, I will set My face against that person and cut him off from his people. Consecrate yourselves therefore, and be holy, for I am the LORD your God." I encourage you to read 1 Samuel chapters 9 through 31 to see how King Saul's life ended after consulting with a medium, along with the consequences of living in disobedience. So as you can see, while I was lost, confused, and in the dark, "His" word was fulfilling itself in my life.

This was the final straw for God with my disobedience, which provoked his anger. Meaning his hands were up and the enemy had full access to rearrange my life. (Jeremiah 4:22) proves that even God's grace runs out. "So that the LORD could no longer bear, because of the evil of your doings, and because of the abominations which ye have committed; therefore is your land a desolation, and an astonishment, and a curse, without an inhabitant, as at this day". This shows that we bring curses on ourselves when we are in disobedience and it gives the enemy free range to take over. So, if you are wondering why you can't keep anything or why your life is in shambles, take a hard look at what you are doing. Let's now discuss the additional doors I opened, including fornication; which opened me up to soul ties formed out of sin along with unexplainable hurt and disillusionment. God intended intimacy to be between a wife and a husband as confirmed in (Hebrews 13:4) "Honor marriage and guard the sacredness of sexual intimacy between wife and husband. God draws a firm line against casual and illicit sex." But the world has completely perverted it with lust.

Or how Idolizing brought iniquities upon my family and me. For God clearly warns us "That we must not make for ourselves an idol of any kind or an image of anything in the heavens or on the earth or in the sea. We must not bow down to them or worship them, for the LORD our God, is a jealous God who will not tolerate our affection for any other gods. He will lay the sins of the parents upon our children, with the entire family being affected. Even children in the third and fourth generations of those who reject him. But he will lavish his unfailing love for a thousand generations on those who love Him and obey His commands" (Exodus 20:4). This shows that our actions can affect our loved ones by being careless and selfish. Truth be told, none of these things, such as crystals, sage, new- age, shrines , celebrities, or people can protect you. The enemy wants you to believe that they can by causing you to become delusional.

God's purpose is for us to have life and live it more abundantly with our trust and total dependency on Him. But as you can see, I chose the world and allowed the thief to come in. To steal, kill and destroy my very existence, or at least try. You see, if I was under the old covenant I would not be in existence today, according (Deuteronomy 7: 11-15). For you had to follow and obey the law in order for his covenant to stay in place. I thank God for the new covenant he has for all us by extending Grace while living unrighteous lives. (Jeremiah 32: 40-42), God makes a promise to us " I will make an everlasting covenant with them: I will never stop doing good for them. I will put a desire in their hearts to worship me, and they will never leave me. I will find joy doing good for them and will faithfully and wholeheartedly replant them in this land. This is what the LORD says: Just as I have brought all these calamities on them, so I will do all the good I have promised them."

At this point, I had no choice but to face the truth and take accountability for my actions with a repenting heart. Trusting in (2 Chronicles 7:14) "If my people who are called by my name humble themselves, and pray and seek my face and turn from their wicked ways, then I will hear from heaven and will forgive their sin and heal their land. " Are you ready to repent so that your land can be healed?

Prayer of Repentance

Lord God, you alone are worthy to be praised, for you have created us by

REPENTANCE

your mighty power. For you have redeemed us by your precious blood, and you hold all things together.

Lord, I know that I have sinned against You, and have acted in rebellious and wicked ways, by turning away from Your commandments and ignoring the truths that are contained throughout the Scripture for my instruction, training in righteousness and well-being.

I have not listened to Your Word and have turned aside from Your voice.. and I have ignored Your many calls to holiness and I stand before You poor and wretched, naked and ashamed.

Lord God, according to Your grace and mercy I ask for Your forgiveness. Keep Your promise to me, Your child I pray.. and wash away my many sins. Help me to put the past behind me and enable me to walk into the future with a desire to do Your will and to live godly in Christ Jesus.

Thank You Lord that Your mercies are new everyday. Thank You that even though I have been so faithless towards You – You have remained faithful towards me. Cleanse my heart from within I pray and renew a right spirit within me, and may I walk in holiness and righteousness from this day forward

Amen!

4

Surrender

Psalms 55:22

***"Give your burdens to the Lord, and he will take care of you. He will not permit the godly to slip and fall."*

L earning to let go and let God was something I heard all the time, as many of us do. However, it was quite tough for me. Given the amount of hurt I experienced throughout my life, such as molestation, abandonment, and rejection, to name a few. It was very difficult to just surrender all of that. But, can I tell you something? "The Lord is close to the broken-hearted; and he rescues those whose spirits are crushed", (Psalm 34:18). Indeed, I was definitely crushed and felt defeated by life as I thought at the time, and I wanted to blame everyone for my problems within my marriage, finances, and relationships . Truth be told, some of the brokenness I experienced was self-inflicted, and yes some were caused by others.

Prior to surrendering to God, I was very isolated from people and situations to protect myself. It was a way for me to try and stop the hurt along with assuming that no one cares. I even convinced myself that if you tried me one time, as I thought. I would just block you on all platforms, like social media and or by phone, and we don't ever have to speak again. But, it didn't work.

SURRENDER

Because the very people I tried to tune out I needed them, and it was not the "Will" of God for me whether family or not. The enemy wanted me to feel like my family and friends did not care about me or respect my feelings. The devil would plant thoughts into my mind that were not of God. Like they don't care if you lived or died, which is not true. (John 10:5)"But they will never follow a stranger; in fact, they will run away from him because they do not recognize a stranger's voice". I understand now why it is so important to read the Bible. "Then we would know the truth, and the truth will set you free",(John 8:32). So, that "we can demolish arguments and every pretension that sets itself up against the knowledge of God, and we take captive every thought to make it obedient to Christ."(2 Corinthians 10:5)

Before coming into the knowledge of His truth, I heard the voice of God whisper so softly to forgive. "Lord what? Do you want me to forgive the very people who have hurt me?" was my response to him. We have all been there where we want to harbor hard feelings in our hearts or plan to get someone back. Can I tell you a little secret? Holding on to grudges only weighs you down and causes all types of health problems. Whenever you take things into your own hands, it never turns out how you intended it to be. "If we forgive those who sin against us, our heavenly Father will forgive us",(Matthew 6 14-15). This was the "Key" to allowing God to begin his work within me. "Surrender your heart to God, turn to him in prayer, and give up your sins— even those you do in secret. Then you won't be ashamed; you will be confident and fearless. Your troubles will go away like water beneath a bridge, and your darkest night will be brighter than noon. You will rest safe and secure, filled with hope and emptied of worry" (Job 11 13-18).

When I surrendered completely, I began to heal emotionally and physically. And this required me to attend church consistently, faith based counseling, serving the community, reading the Bible, prayer, eating right and fellowshipping. This allowed me to hear the Lord even more clearly when he said if you trust me; I will put back the pieces of the puzzle in your life, and I will heal you from the brokenness. So, I received instructions from the Lord to write out everyone's name that I carried an offense with, and to forgive them by writing a letter to myself, and some individuals he actually had me place a call to. This also allowed me to see my mistakes in certain situations. By taking accountability and asking for their forgiveness of my actions. You may be wondering if I received an apology for the things I felt offended by with people. A few individuals apologized, and I had some that did not feel any remorse. And that's okay because I was finally able to release it and not hold it inside. Talk about the level of peace I received by not holding on to unnecessary baggage because I trusted in his "Will" along with resting in him. For the Lord said "Peace I leave with you; my peace I give you. I do not give to you as the world gives. Do not let your hearts be troubled and do not be afraid" (John 14:27).

Yeah, I know it can be difficult at times, and I didn't say it would be easy on this journey. So remember, "For we wrestle not against flesh and blood, but against principalities, against powers, against the rulers of the darkness of this world, against spiritual wickedness in high places", (Ephesians 6:12). I encourage you to always seek God for peace and to have a forgiving heart in every situation or circumstance. Also, ask God to show you his perspective in every situation, and "Trust in the Lord with all your heart and lean not on your own understanding;But in all your ways submit to Him, and He will make your paths straight" (Proverbs 3 5-6). Are you ready to surrender?

Prayer to Surrender

I surrender myself completely to You, Lord. You are always faithful and You extend Your grace to me constantly, even when I do not realize it. I claim Your promise of forgiveness and cleansing in its fullness. In faith, I receive the victory today that you have already put in place for me. I do this in the name of Your Son Jesus Christ, my Savior with a grateful heart.
Amen!

5

Foundation

Matthew 7:24-27

"Anyone who listens to my teaching and follows it is wise, like a person who builds a house on solid rock. Though the rain comes in torrents and the floodwaters rise and the winds beat against that house, it won't collapse because it is built on bedrock. But anyone who hears my teaching and doesn't obey it is foolish, like a person who builds a house on sand. When the rains and floods come and the winds beat against that house, it will collapse with a mighty crash."

Discovering my foundation was faulty required me to rebuild on Christ. By establishing the right mindset, heart posture, and by consuming the word of God daily. Recognizing that the hand of God was crippled as long I remained worldly and not a Spiritual Christian. Through this transition, I had a burning desire to get to know God and understand his "Will" for my life. I've always questioned how would I know what his "Will" is for me or my purpose. In order for me to find out, I understood quickly that I had to read his word as I walked in Christ knowing that we are his special possession. So, I began to search for a Christian Bible that was suitable for me to comprehend. Like most of us, sometimes we need it to be plain and clear. It is understood that reading "thou art" throws a lot of us off. And God completely understands this while meeting us at the level we are currently on. He never wants us to compete or be like someone else, because we are all made with uniqueness, setting us apart as individuals. As I began to read his word my mindset started to shift as I no longer thought the same. You see, as long as I thought of hatred, violence ,being unwanted etc. It became my reality and what I attracted from others. Because I did not have the Holy Spirit and word within me. "For as he thinks in his heart, so is he in behavior, one who manipulates. He says to you, "Eat and drink,"Yet his heart is not with you but it is begrudging the cost", (Proverbs 23:7).

Okay, let me break it down. God is love and If I hold hate in my heart, it is because I dislike something about my life, holding on to Unforgiveness and or it was taught, creating jealousy, envy, and strife. But, if you take it to God on how you are feeling thus putting your flesh into subjection."He will give you a new heart, and put a new spirit in you. Taking out your stony, stubborn heart and give you a tender, responsive heart. And he will put his Spirit in you so that you will follow his decrees and be careful to obey his regulations", (Ezekiel 36:26). This is why it's so important that we allow God to work on us - to dismantle our ways of thinking and restore our hearts from brokenness, along with removing anything that is not of Him while becoming more like Him. He loves us, and as His children, we should be displaying the same. Whew, can I tell you it took me years to learn that love is an action and not a feeling. "For he commands us too: Love one another. In the same way he has loved us, by loving one another. This is how everyone will recognize that you are his disciples—when they see the love you have for each other" (John 13:34).

God promises that "He will keep us in perfect peace whose mind stays on him, because we trust in Him" (Isaiah 26:3), along with conditioning our hearts that are forgiving, filled with love despite circumstances. Slowly, God began to walk me through deliverance of healing from depression, trauma and any other hurt that I've ever experienced. He also gave me direction on how to renounce everything that I was attached to with Satan and his kingdom . Let me give you an example of why: If you have ever paid a fortune teller, you have just entered into a contract with Satan, and whatever that fortune teller is attached to, has now attached itself to you spiritually. In addition to lying, cheating , stealing, fornication and any other sinful nature creating open doors that give him further access, which needs to be shut immediately once you become knowledgeable of where things took a turn in your life. This process allowed God to restore my foundation of Christ, built on a rock and not sinking sand. Where I'm no longer double- minded but stabled in who I am in Christ. "But when you ask, you must believe and not doubt, because the one who doubts is like a wave of the sea, blown and tossed by the wind. That person should not expect to receive anything from the Lord. Such a person is double-minded and unstable in all they do", (James 1 7-8). Are you ready to reset your foundation?

Prayer for Foundation
Father in God in the name of Jesus Christ, we ask You to help us to embrace the reason that we must apply Your teachings to our lives – so that our foundation will be unshakable and storm-proof when the howling winds and surging rains beat against us. The foundation of this world is temporal and growing more and more decadent, so we choose instead to build our lives on the eternal foundation of Your Holy Word, as You teach us all throughout Scripture. We will come to regret that which consumed our heart, our mind and our time in building temporal foundations, but we will never come to regret building a spiritual foundation composed of Jesus Christ and His eternal worth. Keep us clear minded and focused so that we are aware of the difference between that which only satisfies us here and that which satisfies for all eternity.
Amen!

6

Restructured

Romans 5 3-5

"Not only that, but we rejoice in our sufferings, knowing that suffering produces endurance, and endurance produces character, and character produces hope, and hope does not put us to shame, because God's love has been poured into our hearts through the Holy Spirit who has been given to us."

Once I relinquished control and trusted in God's "Will", my character began to be restructured by me allowing and accepting the Holy Spirit to prune and lead me in every area of my life. You see "He cuts off every branch of us that doesn't bear grapes. And every branch that is grape-bearing he prunes it back to its original state so that it will bear even more", (John 15:2). This pushes us back into the message spoken by our Heavenly Father over our lives. For he knew us before we were formed in our mother's womb (Jeremiah 1:5), and he knows that we are not perfect and that we are going to have stumbling blocks. But the "Key" is to not allow it to become an anchor that hinders your walk in Christ, weighing you down.

Through this process of transformation, I began to become into alignment with the image of God. Where my flesh was no longer ruler over me. With the

Holy Spirit now in control, I was able to operate in the fruits of the spirit. Are you wondering what that is? Well, let me tell you. "The Holy Spirit produces in us love, joy, peace, patience, kindness, goodness, faithfulness, gentleness, and self-control", (Galatians 5:22). That requires you to deny yourself and pick up your cross to follow our Lord and Savior, (Matthew 6:24). When you pick up your cross, you are picking up the ways of God. Where you are now constantly dying to yourself daily by trusting with God's understanding, and this is the benefit of the Holy Spirit that resides in us, knowing right from wrong.

Experiencing the love of God cannot be matched or compared to any human being. Ask yourself: What person do you know will send their son to die for our sins? The answer will be no one. That's the kind of God we serve. God showed his great love for us by sending Christ to die for us while we were still sinners. Because of his love shown towards me, I was able to show others in return. Prior to Christ, I used to be so cold-hearted, stubborn and shut off towards people because trust was broken and this was rooted in not experiencing the love of my parents. Then God reminded me where I went wrong. Which was searching for love in all the wrong places while being rejected by partners, family, parents and friends because of my expectations. I wanted them to love me so desperately and provide the love I was giving in return till the point I lost myself. But God said try me, and I will not reject you nor will you have to beg. For he tells us, "It is better to trust in the "Him" Than to put confidence in man", (Psalms 146:3). In order for you to show love, drop the expectation and place your trust in God, who will not waver as man does. This will allow you to show love unconditionally despite it all.

We all have seasons where there is either grief, heartache, disappointments and or loss, which can be very detrimental. But the Lord says count it all joy. "For he is the Father of all mercy! God of all healing counsel! He comes alongside us when we go through hard times with comfort, and before you know it, he brings us alongside someone else who is going through hard times so that we can be there for that person just as God was there for us"(

2 Corinthians 1 3-5). This is the part I had to understand, because by no means is it easy. At times you will feel like your life is crumbling, and that could be true. But you have to remember, it's not about you, as it is far greater than you. I'm not saying you shouldn't cry or feel. For He knows that we have feelings; but it is what you do with those feelings that determines the outcome. I've learned to just cry out to God when I feel the heaviness, with me placing all of my burdens at His feet. Then, I pull it back together and press through. So, have that moment to feel. But, don't stay there. Instead, praise Him with Joy and confidence that every season has an ending before a shift takes place. "There is a time for everything, and a season for every activity under the heavens: a time to be born and a time to die, a time to plant and a time to uproot, a time to kill and a time to heal, a time to tear down and a time to build, a time to weep and a time to laugh, a time to mourn and a time to dance, a time to scatter stones and a time to gather them, a time to embrace and a time to refrain from embracing, a time to search and a time to give up, a time to keep and a time to throw away, a time to tear and a time to mend, a time to be silent and a time to speak, a time to love and a time to hate, a time for war and a time for peace" (Ecclesiastes 3 1-8).

I used to say I needed peace in my life. How many of us say this on a daily basis? But yet there is still confusion and conflict circulating all around you. At times I would drink, thinking it would ease or bring comfort. But it only made the situation worse, because the problem did not go anywhere along with a nasty hangover. Now, as I walk in Christ I have unexplainable peace, knowing that I may go through some things; but this time it's different because God is with me and I no longer need to drink to suppress my emotions. Instead I grab the word of God to remind myself of what is true and never changes. For He tells us "Have no anxiety at all, but in everything, by prayer and petition, with thanksgiving, make your requests known to God. Then the peace of God that surpasses all understanding will guard your hearts and minds in Christ Jesus", (Philippians 4 6-7). As you can see peace comes from God and not from the World.

It was a habit to say whatever I felt without remorse. Because, to me, it is about keeping it real, or a hundred, as some may say. However , we don't realize how deadly our mouths are. "For death and life are in the power of the tongue, and those who love it will eat its fruit", (Proverbs 18:21). Basically, whatever you speak is what you will experience. Such as conflict, anger, confusion, curses, gossip, drama etc. I had to learn and ask God for wisdom on when to speak, how to speak, and when not to speak, along with what I speak over myself. This allowed the Holy Spirit to show me how to be more gentle, kind, and good towards others. There is nothing more unappealing than a person with a bad attitude, no filter, and lack of self control. Sometimes, you have to pull out that mirror and look at yourself. This could answer some questions about why you have issues with others. "Pleasant words are like a honeycomb, sweet to the soul, and health to the bones", (Proverbs 16:24).

Waiting on the Lord requires patience. I would pray and expect it to happen immediately. And, then question the Lord what is taking so long or if He even heard my prayer. Until I read(2 Peter 3:8) "But do not forget this one thing, dear friends: With the Lord a day is like a thousand years, and a thousand years are like a day." This scripture humbled me and corrected my attitude while waiting all at the same time. Yes, he wants to give us the desires of our hearts." For He knows the plans He has for us," declares the LORD, "plans to prosper us and not to harm us. With plans to give us hope and a future", (Jeremiah 29:11). So, It may take some time to see your prayer answered or He just wants the best for you according to His plans. I encourage you to keep praying, seek Him and He will show you. This will also teach you how to be patient with others as it did for me.

Our faithfulness to God means trusting in Him and loving Him through all circumstances. It means following His commandments even when the world does otherwise. This shows God your loyalty and prevents you from being double-minded about who He is. This is how God develops your character, empowers you to do His works, and transforms you into a new person, operating in the fruits of the Spirit. Are you ready for the Holy Spirit to take over so that you can be restructured thus forming your character?

Prayer on Restructuring Character
Dear, Heavenly Father
I come to you asking you to Create in me a clean heart and renew a right spirit within me. That I will operate and grow in love, joy, peace, patience, kindness, goodness, faithfulness, gentleness, and self-control everyday you allow me to live as long as I have breath in my body. Cast me not away from your presence O God and take not your Holy Spirit from me.
Restore to me the joy of your salvation and uphold me with a willing spirit. Lord, open my lips,and my mouth that I will praise you always despite life circumstances.
And I declare and decree that I'm moving in victory. With a faithful heart and unwavering mind. Because greater is he in me than the world.
Amen!

7

Faith

James 1 2-4

"Dear brothers and sisters, when troubles of any kind come your way, consider it an opportunity for great joy. For you know that when your faith is tested, your endurance has a chance to grow. So let it grow, for when your endurance is fully developed, you will be perfect and complete, needing nothing."

When you are in a season of your faith being tested, it requires that you are obeying fully with a humbled, surrendered heart to God. This phase of my life was the most difficult time. You may ask why. Well, some was due to my disobedience while living in sin, which caused me to lose some things amongst having to trust God, with my marriage, daughter, parents, and family. You see, like most, we think that once we submit to God all of our problems go away. But that is further from the truth. Yes, God celebrates us when we turn and walk upright. But there are consequences to our actions. In addition to our "Father" restoring and fixing what has been broken to bring it back into alignment. I remember crying out to God to save my marriage and relationships at the end of 2020. He said, "I understand your frustration, but you are going to go through this, and it will be my way."

I understood at that moment that it would take maturity in Christ, especially my attitude and how I handled situations. God allowed my husband and me to separate to get my attention and work on me. Was it easy? No, I was devastated. He said, "If you trust me and have faith, I will restore what you have lost and put the puzzle pieces back together again." God was reminding me of what He had promised. At the time, I couldn't see it because my husband and I were at odds, distant from family members, and my relationship with my daughter was deteriorating. God tested me to see if I would trust Him in restoring my marriage and relationships. Isn't it amazing how God knows what will get your attention?

This phase of my life required me to pray without ceasing, have patience, fast and walk by faith without looking at the natural. You may hear someone say. I prayed once, and I gave it to God. Or It was not a part of the Lord's "Will". No, you gave up without hearing God's response, and at times it could mean waiting for the Lord's best for you. (1 Thessalonians 5:17) reminds us to keep praying. So I knew if I stopped praying, the devil would have the upper hand and think that he had won. When God promised in (1 John 4:4) "You are of God, little children, and have overcome them, because He who is in you is greater than he who is in the world". This means that we already have victory because of the Holy Spirit that resides in us. In the midst of trial and tribulation, God began to bring me and my family members close to heal and resolve issues of misunderstandings. Without me realizing that God was giving me precious time to spend with my baby brother that I have lost. Due to selfishness and stubbornness, I missed out on so much time.

At the beginning of 2021, my brother began to experience a mental breakdown, and I felt that he was misunderstood. He too was going through a separation from his wife. So, I was able to identify the devil and his tricks head-on. For it was no coincidence that we were both going through the same thing. This was a generational curse trying to take its course in both of our lives. Shortly after, my brother could not be located and it started to take its toll on me, my family, and especially my mother. This is a reminder that

FAITH

although a parent may not be close or have a relationship with their children it does not stop the hurt of seeing their child go through painful situations.

One day as I was fellowshipping with other believers who were my disciple sisters. A leader asked if there were any prayer requests. Usually , I'm the person who will not ask or sit quietly. But that day I felt led to. I expressed what happened and that my prayer was that he would be found and home before his birthday. And let me tell you because of Faith and others touching and agreeing with me. The Lord showed up and exceeded far more than I could ever imagine. Soon after, my mother received a phone call seven days later from an unknown caller, a complete stranger. She stated do you have a son by this name and explained that he was in another state.

Now, here is the kicker. Another stranger who was associated with the young lady who called my mom was her boss. He said we will take care of him; just fly down and I will purchase tickets to fly all three of you back home. Not only that, the way my family pulled together amazed me. Do you see how God was working? He had his hands all over this. And guess what? My brother made it home before December 24, which was his birthday, and we took pictures under the Christmas tree. This is a reminder to me that God will move the hearts of his children and that we are entertaining Angels right here on earth without even noticing it. You may have heard the old saying: be careful how you treat people because you never know if that person could be the answer to your prayers.

In between this time, the Lord restored my marriage two years to the exact date we were separated. At times I would question God, just like Gideon. Lord, is this my Husband? And He would answer yes. So although we were apart, I still had to pray for him and respect him despite it all. The Lord told me you will show agape love to my son. Of course, I was like really. Well, your son isn't showing anything so why me? But this is where I had to truly push my pride to the side. And it actually helped me grow as a mature Christian. Along with understanding my role as a wife by respecting my husband as the head of our home. As you can see the Lord was restoring order.

A couple months later, my brother went missing again. And my husband said the Lord showed me you will see your brother again. Now, like most, I said, Oh sure, the Lord told you that, huh? But, the Lord showed me to not doubt his son. Two months later, while we were volunteering, I heard my husband's name being yelled out. And, guess who it was - my brother. What struck me the most was that my brother had not seen my husband in years, yet he knew it was him.You see, I never stopped praying for him. And God showed up and covered him again in December, right before his birthday.

Before things took a turn, God gave me two beautiful birthdays to share with my brother. One night, as I was sleeping, I woke up with the need to breathe. I kept telling my husband I feel like I'm helping someone breathe. Well, it was my brother who was in the hospital. Come to find out he walked all the way there and admitted himself in, where he was placed on life support. I could not let my faith go that he would pull through. When he didn't, I felt like I dropped the ball in my prayers, and my faith was shaken to its core. I asked the Lord why. He told me I needed to be at peace with this and know that my brother was at peace. Grief nearly took over my life for months. Until I made a decision that I had to get out of this by being around other believers that would push me through to keep going.

You may be wondering if I have a relationship with my parents. As I touched on it lightly. The answer would be no. But it does not stop my love for them, honor, faith, or prayers that the Lord will make it right. Our parents have gone through things as well that could have affected their parenting. We have to respect that they have experienced situations without truly healing. So give them grace and room to recognize and heal. But I'm happy that my beautiful daughter and I have grown tremendously. For the Lord told me you have to let her live and stop trying to control. He also reminded me of how I was when growing up. So, parents, allow your children to take on their own identity and trust that you've done your best raising them to be great women and men of God. Sharing my experiences while walking in Faith was not easy. It is to show you that things may happen to throw you off course. But the "Key" is to never stop trusting and believing in God if you want to see His "Hand" in your life, once you accept Christ as your Lord and Savior, repent, surrender, build foundation, and allow the "Holy Spirit" to guide you while holding on to your faith for an amazing transformation.

Prayer Of Faith

Dear Heavenly Father, Thank you for building our endurance while going through unpleasant or difficult situations without giving up. We thank you, Lord , for giving us stamina to remain steadfast and unmovable in our Faith. Lord, thank you that we are not double- minded, but stable in our minds. We thank you, Lord, that you are a rewarder of those who diligently seek you. For your word reminds us, according to (Hebrews 11:6), that it is impossible to please you without Faith. So we will press wholeheartedly as your children in Christ fully armored, holding the shield of Faith trusting in you. Amen!

8

Dedication

To my Heavenly Father , thank you for giving me a fresh start in life and wisdom to write this book. All that I am and all that I shall become, I owe it to you.

To my husband, my daughter, brother, family and friends. May the Lord bless you for all the love and support you have given me.

To my dearest late brother, thank you for always loving me as your sister. You will always be remembered, loved and cherished.

I am also thankful to all those who have played various roles in my life at various stages, no matter how small, to make it possible. May the good Lord who knows each of you by name bless all of you and grant you your heart desires as you continue to delight in Him.

www.ingramcontent.com/pod-product-compliance
Lightning Source LLC
Chambersburg PA
CBHW070859050426
42453CB00012B/2271